52
nature craft
projects

52
nature craft projects

BARBORA KURCOVA

THUNDER BAY
P·R·E·S·S
San Diego, California

Thunder Bay Press
An imprint of Printers Row Publishing Group
10350 Barnes Canyon Road, Suite 100
San Diego, CA 92121
www.thunderbaybooks.com
mail@thunderbaybooks.com

Printers Row Publishing Group is a division of Readerlink Distribution
Services, LLC. Thunder Bay Press is a registered trademark of
Readerlink Distribution Services, LLC.

Correspondence regarding the content of this book should be sent to
Thunder Bay Press, Editorial Department, at the above address. All
other correspondence (author inquiries, permissions) concerning the
content of this book should be addressed to Quarto Publishing plc.

Conceived, edited, and designed by
Quarto Publishing plc,
6 Blundell Street, London, N7 9BH, UK.

QUAR.328357

Thunder Bay Press
Publisher: Peter Norton • Associate Publisher: Ana Parker
Editor: Dan Mansfield
Senior Product Manager: Kathryn C. Dalby

Quarto Publishing
Designer: Elisa Rocchi
Deputy Art Director: Martina Calvio
Art Director: Gemma Wilson
Senior Editor: Kate Burkett
Publisher: Samantha Warrington

Library of Congress Control Number: 2019954624

ISBN: 978-1-64517-244-4

Printed in Singapore

24 23 22 21 20 1 2 3 4 5

MIX
Paper from
responsible sources
FSC® C016973

Meet Barbora

Hello, nature lovers!

I am so happy you are holding my book in your hands, and I can't wait to spend the whole year crafting together. I have always been a nature collector and often find acorns, conkers, feathers, and the like in my coat pockets. They are tiny joys I find on the way to and from work, and never fail to brighten my day.

I am originally from the Czech Republic but moved to Norway in 2014. At the time, creativity was a much-needed escape in a difficult life situation. As the budget was tight, I started to look outside my door for creative material, which opened a whole new world for me. Suddenly, I wasn't just collecting—the treasures I found started to become something more.

Now I can't imagine living my creative life without nature. The change of the seasons brings exciting materials, colors, and textures into my photography and home. What I love about using nature for creating and decorating is that it is widely accessible and affordable for everyone. No matter if you live in a town or in the countryside, there is always a patch of land to explore and bring back treasures. I am also passionate about sustainability, and using nature as much as you can is a way to be more conscious of our planet.

I only ask you to be respectful of the natural world around you once you start foraging for your materials. There are just three simple rules to follow: If it is on the ground, take as much as you like. If it is alive, take as much as you need. If it is behind someone's fence—don't even think about it!

I hope you will have a great year enjoying every season fully, observing changes in nature, and cherishing the small gifts we get from her, every single day!

WINTER

1

Nature print paper,
page 12

2

Walnut wreath,
page 14

3

Bird feeder,
page 16

4

Pine cone garland,
page 18

5

Twig letter,
page 20

6

Twig stars,
page 22

7

Nature wrapping,
page 24

8

Advent calendar,
page 26

9

Picture frame,
page 28

10

Pine cone
decorations,
page 29

11

Angel,
page 30

12

Winter wreath,
page 32

13

Frozen lantern,
page 34

SPRING

14

Leaf pounding,
page 40

15

Egg holder,
page 44

16

Nature brushes,
page 46

17

Spring wreath,
page 48

18

Nature eggs,
page 52

19

Buttercup chandelier,
page 54

20

Clay print,
page 58

21

Egg planter,
page 60

22

Fern print,
page 62

23

Feather bouquet,
page 64

24

Tiny terrarium,
page 66

25

Nature display,
page 68

26

Seed balls,
page 70

SUMMER

27 Flower pressing, page 76

28 Printing with shells, page 80

29 Floral garland, page 82

30 Dreamcatcher, page 84

31 Twig heart, page 88

32 Pressed flowers candle, page 90

33 Forever bouquet, page 92

34 Shell wall hanging, page 94

35 Flower crown, page 96

36 Shell candles, page 98

37 Pressed flowers card, page 100

38 Pebble game, page 102

39 Floral lampshade, page 104

FALL

40

Acorn mushrooms,
page 110

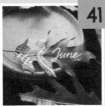

41

Drawing on leaves,
page 112

42

Rowan hearts,
page 114

43

Apple garland,
page 116

44

Halloween mask,
page 118

45

Leaf mobile,
page 120

46

Simple fall wreath,
page 122

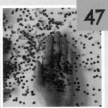

47

Nature confetti,
page 124

48

Leafy crown,
page 126

49

Preserving leaves,
page 128

50

Leaf roses,
page 130

51

Leaf-shaped trinket
dish, page 134

52

Conker wreath,
page 138

CHAPTER

WINTER

NATURE PRINT PAPER

TOOLS AND MATERIALS
- Brown wrapping paper
- Acorns
- Fir branches
- Washi tape or paper weights
- Ribbon or string

Brown paper for gift wrapping has been my favorite for many years. However, every year I try to find a way to personalize the wrapping for someone special. This time, I used items from nature as decorative stamps—and I just love the results. I used acorn hats to print circles, acorn bodies to make dots, and fir branches for a foliage effect.

And then, it is as easy as it looks: just dip the object into some paint and stamp the paper in an organized or disorganized manner. To keep the paper still and flat while you do this, it is a good idea to weigh it down with something or tape it to the table with some washi tape, which will not ruin the paper itself.

WALNUT WREATH

Creating Christmas decorations with natural materials is a big tradition in Scandinavia, where I come from. This walnut wreath is a great way to use leftover walnut shells after baking delicious Christmas cookies. Either display the wreath as a table centerpiece or create smaller versions to decorate your Christmas tree.

TOOLS AND MATERIALS
- Walnuts
- Small knife
- Strong craft glue
- Twine
- Ribbon

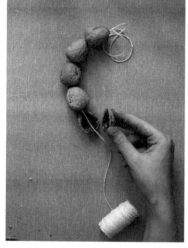

1 First you need to empty the walnuts. Using a small knife, place the tip of the blade into the bottom seam of the walnut. Carefully wiggle the knife until the walnut opens. If the walnuts do not split straight down the seam, don't worry, as you will glue the halves back together again later. Scrape out the contents of the walnuts so you have empty shells.

2 To create the wreath, apply glue all the way around one half of a shell. Place the twine on top, so that it bisects the shell vertically, then press the other half of the shell on top, aligning it as best as you can with the first half. Repeat with all the walnuts, making sure each shell is butted up close to the previous one until you have a row of seven or eight shells.

3 Create a circle with the shells, then tie the ends of the twine securely to make a small, neat wreath. Decorate the finished wreath at the top with a ribbon tied into a bow.

If you are intending to hang the wreath, leave the ends of the twine longer and tie them into a hanging loop at the top.

BIRD FEEDER

Winter is a time of giving back to nature, so I always like to create some nutritious bird food to place outside when it's cold. If you are lucky enough to have a garden, and you use the right seed and nut mixture, you can attract the most beautiful birds and have the best view from your window.

TOOLS AND MATERIALS

- Aluminum foil
- Cookie cutter
- Bird-friendly seeds and nuts
- Coconut oil
- Pitcher, plate, and spoon
- Toothpick or barbecue stick
- Natural twine

1 Create the main structure of the feeder from aluminum foil. Choose a cookie cutter in the shape you would like your bird feeder to be, then place it in the center of the foil. Wrap the foil over the shape, making sure there are no gaps. Remove the cookie cutter and reshape the foil to create a mold for the shape of your feeder.

2 Next, prepare the food mixture. Gather your selection of seeds and nuts. If it is not already liquid, gently melt some coconut oil in a microwave or over a pan of simmering water. Pour the liquid oil into a pitcher.

3 Add a mixture of the seeds and nuts to the pitcher, then place the aluminum mold on a plate. Pour the mixture from the pitcher into the foil mold until it is about three-quarters of the way up. Use a spoon to make sure the mold is filled nicely. Push a toothpick or barbecue stick through the mixture near the top of the feeder to create a tiny hole for hanging with twine. Refrigerate for 24 hours to allow the oil—and the feeder—to set.

Once ready, peel off the aluminum mold and thread some twine through the hole to hang the bird feeder. If you decide to hang the feeder in the wild, make sure to use 100 percent natural twine, so you don't pollute nature with plastic material. As the food is for smaller birds, it is advisable to hang the feeder inside the bushes to provide protection from crows.

PINE CONE GARLAND

TOOLS AND MATERIALS
- Pine cones
- Twine

Pine cones are some of the most accessible natural props you can find at this time of year. You can collect lots of different sizes and easily create a pretty garland. I often grab two or three pine cones on the way home from work, and by the end of the week I have enough for a craft project of some kind.

You can tie the pine cones just next to each other with cotton twine, or leave small gaps. Simply wrap the twine around the middle of the pine cone, make a knot or two, and continue until you reach the length you want. Then hang the garland around a window frame or from a shelf, or even use it as a festive chain for a Christmas tree.

TWIG LETTER

If you want to try a modern take on the traditional wreath, you can mold some twigs into the shape of your favorite letter. Not overly difficult in comparison with creating a conventional wreath, the letter can also be decorated according to the season or mood, creating a great wall decoration or party ornament.

TOOLS AND MATERIALS
- Bendy twigs (not too dry)
- Florist's wire or other craft wire
- Hand pruners or sharp scissors
- Green foliage
- Berries or flowers

1 Prepare the twigs first. Depending on your choice of letter, select straight, firm twigs for the straight parts of the letter and fresher, more bendy twigs for the rounded shapes. For now, you only need the thicker twigs to prepare the main framework of the letter. The bigger the letter, the thicker the twigs you will need to hold the shape. Simply twist a few of the thicker twigs together to create the main framework of the letter.

2 Cut the wire into 4-inch lengths. Take a few of the more bendy twigs, braid them to make them more stable, and then gently bend them. Choose the point of connection and secure with wire wrapped around the main stem and the connecting twigs in an X shape. Set the foundation of the letter with just a few twigs and then add in more layers. Cut off any ends that are sticking out.

3 Once the framework is done, you can add whatever decoration you like—perhaps foliage, plus berries in winter and flowers in spring. Attach the decoration with lengths of wire, in the same way as you did the twigs. You can either decorate one corner or cover the whole frame. To make this easier, cut small bunches of greenery and berries or flowers. By going in one direction, from the bottom to the top, for example, you can cover all the wire connections.

TWIG STARS

These twig stars are a super-easy way to decorate your home, and you need very few supplies to make them. You can leave the stars bare, paint them, or use glitter or tape to add your own personal style. The stars can be hung one by one, or you can create a small display by hanging them all together on a larger branch.

TOOLS AND MATERIALS

- 5 twigs per star
- Hand pruners or sharp scissors
- Twine
- Yarn or ribbon

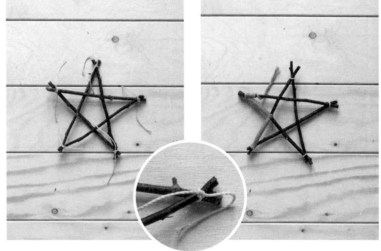

1 Prepare the twigs by cutting them all to the same length. You will need five twigs for each star. For smaller stars, you don't want the twigs to be too thick or bendy. The bigger the star, the thicker the twigs should be.

2 Arrange the twigs in a star shape on a flat surface, alternating the twigs over and under one another, as shown. Use small lengths of twine to tie the twigs together at each point.

3 Now your star is ready to be decorated. Cut the yarn or ribbon into small lengths. Take one length and tie it to one of the five points to secure it. Wrap the length of yarn or ribbon around one twig until it runs out, then take another length and connect it to the previous one with a knot and continue as before. Wrap around both twigs where they overlap. Repeat until all the twigs are covered, leaving the hexagon shape in the center of the star exposed.

NATURE WRAPPING

This is my absolute favorite way to wrap presents for Christmas. Once you've learned the basic method, you can also use this wrapping for birthday presents, housewarming gifts, and much more. It is also a great way to use all of those little trinkets from nature you collected over the fall, such as pine cones, feathers, and leaves. Why not add a little card or note to make each gift that bit more personal?

TOOLS AND MATERIALS
- Natural brown paper
- Scissors
- Sticky tape
- Nature finds, such as pine cones, feathers, and leaves
- Name tag, card, ribbon, or twine

1 Choose the gift you want to wrap (a book is great to start with for practice), and cut the paper to about three times the length and width.

2 Put your gift to one side. Fold the bottom of the paper up to meet the top, then fold the top half of the top layer back down toward the bottom of the paper.

3 Wrap your gift as normal, making sure the pocket fold is on the outside of the wrapping. Tuck the ends of the pocket to the back of the gift and tape them in place. Decorate the little pocket any way you like by tucking some nature finds inside—branches, acorns, dried grass, leaves, or feathers are all good choices. Add a name tag, card, ribbon, or twine as a finishing touch.

TIP
Once you understand the basic method, you can make the pocket smaller or bigger, depending on the size of the objects you wish to use as decoration!

ADVENT CALENDAR

Although I don't have children, I have always made advent calendars for my friends or myself. December can be really dark and daunting in Norway, so having a little joy every morning to cheer your spirits can be exactly what you need to set you up for the day ahead. This advent calendar uses natural resources and also reuses materials such as leftover fabrics, gift wrap, and old book pages. It can easily be adjusted in terms of both size and style to fit any room.

TOOLS AND MATERIALS

- 6 fairly thick twigs of increasing size
- Thin rope or thick twine
- Scissors
- 24 small gifts and letters
- Fabric, gift wrap, old books
- Twine or ribbon
- Greeting cards and gift tags

1 Collect six twigs of increasing size (you may need to trim them down). I kept the bark on my twigs because I like a rustic look, but if your home is more minimalist, then you can peel the bark off or paint the twigs to suit your decor. Arrange the twigs on your work surface in ascending order.

2 You now need to join the twigs together with rope or twine. I had two lengths of macramé rope, so I used those. Using one length of rope or twine, and starting from the top and working downward, tie a knot on the left-hand end of each twig. Repeat on the right-hand side with the other length of rope or twine. I did this step on the floor because it made it easier to keep the distances between the twigs the same. Tie the lengths of rope or twine together at the top.

3 Finally, it's time to start hanging the small gifts and letters. I used leftover fabric, gift wrap, and pages from old books to wrap my gifts. Use twine or ribbon to hang the gifts and letters, as well as some greeting cards and gift tags, from each branch.

The finished advent calendar will decorate your room for a whole season, so make sure to use colors and materials that you enjoy looking at. You might also like to add a few Christmas decorations or even some Christmas lights. It can be fun to number the presents and create a treasure hunt for children, too.

PICTURE FRAME

TOOLS AND MATERIALS

- 4 straight(ish) twigs
- Hand pruners or sharp scissors
- Hot-glue gun or strong craft glue
- String or craft wire

If you often find yourself with lots of postcards, nice pictures, or children's drawings and are not sure how to display them, making a simple and affordable picture frame out of twigs is a great solution. You can customize the frame to your liking in terms of size or color by cutting or painting the wood. I think this is a particularly good idea if you want to gift someone drawings by you or your children.

To make the frame, you need four straight(ish) twigs—the smaller the frame, the thinner the twigs can be, as they will manage to hold themselves well. Cut the four twigs to the right length, so they will fit together nicely when you arrange them in a rectangle or square to create the frame. You can keep the bark on for a rustic look. Then use either strong craft glue or a hot-glue gun to secure the twigs firmly at all four meeting points.

Once the glue has dried, paint the whole frame if you wish to add a pop of color. Cut your artwork to size and glue it to the back of the frame. Then tie a short piece of string or wire to the top twig so you can hang the picture later.

PINE CONE DECORATIONS

TOOLS AND MATERIALS

- Pine cones
- Twine or florist's wire
- Hot-glue gun or strong craft glue
- Old jar or glass (optional)
- Acrylic paint or liquid craft paint (optional)

In my opinion, pine cones belong on a Christmas tree and are already beautiful decorations in themselves. If you collected a few pine cones during the fall, you can use them now to decorate your tree.

To suspend each pine cone, take a length of twine or florist's wire and fold it in half to create a hanging loop. Use a hot-glue gun or some strong craft glue to stick the ends of the twine or wire to the bottom of the pine cone (where it was originally attached to the tree branch). You can then hang the pine cone from a branch.

The pine cones look beautiful as they are, but it is easy to give them a touch of color. Find an old jar or glass large enough for you to fit the pine cone in, then fill it with a mixture of acrylic paint and water—about two parts paint to one part water—or just use some liquid craft paint. The paint should be "thick," but still slightly runny. Then, holding the pine cone by the loop, dip it into the paint until it is well covered. Remove the pine cone from the paint, let dry, and hang on the tree.

ANGEL

There are so many ways to create Christmas decorations, and avoid buying new or plastic gifts. This sweet angel reminds me of children singing Christmas carols. You can make one or a whole group, and then hang on the Christmas tree or a branch. You could also create a little scene on your festive table. The fun thing about this project is that you can really play with the colors and accessories, and, if you make more than one, each angel can look a little different.

TOOLS AND MATERIALS
- 2 small feathers
- Acorn
- Acrylic paints and paintbrush
- Black marker pen
- Pine cone
- Hot-glue gun or strong craft glue
- Yarn or ribbon (optional)

1 If you already have nice white feathers for the wings, or don't mind them being a bit colored, you can skip this step. However, if you'd prefer perfectly white feathers, paint them with some white acrylic paint.

2 Paint the acorn to make the head of your angel. I used a very pale pink, but, if you're making more than one angel, you can use different colors and have a very diverse choir. Once the head is dry, paint the "hat." I chose black, but just use any color you like. You could also paint the hat with more than one color, or add dots, stripes, or other patterns.

3 To create the angel's face, use the black marker pen to draw two simple "U" shapes to symbolize closed eyes and draw an "O" for a singing mouth. You might also like to add other features, such as red cheeks, eyebrows, or eyelashes.

4 Now glue the acorn head to the pine-cone body. I removed a small section at the top of my pine cone to make more space for the head. I used a hot-glue gun, but you can also use a strong craft glue that turns transparent when dry. In both cases, hold the head in place for a while to let the glue dry a bit.

5 Finally, you can add the angel's wings. Trim the feathers as short as necessary to make the wings look nice. I used rather big feathers because I wanted the ends to be wider and more "wing-like." Trim the bottom part of each feather and then glue to the back of the pine cone by inserting into one of the layers and adding some glue. If you would like to suspend your angel, glue a looped piece of yarn or ribbon to the back of the head.

WINTER WREATH

TOOLS AND MATERIALS

- Soft, bendy twigs, such as birch or willow
- Fir branches
- Hand pruners or sharp scissors
- Colorful decorations, such as red-and-white twine and acorn mushrooms
- Florist's wire or other craft wire

Have you seen the spring wreath (see page 48)? You can make a winter version by following the same instructions, but simply replace the flowers and green leaves with fir branches and Christmas decorations. I used red-and-white twine tied into bows, as well as homemade acorn mushrooms (see page 110), but you can use anything you like.

You can usually buy a branch of fir tree from the garden center or a Christmas market. The places that sell Christmas trees also sometimes give them away for free, as they often cut off small branches when shaping the trees. Alternatively, you can go to the woods and gently take a few.

FROZEN LANTERN

Light is very important during the winter in Norway. The days are long and dark, and so decorating with different kinds of lights has become a big tradition. This frozen lantern is wonderful for decorating your porch or balcony in winter, and can be a great way to welcome guests to a winter party. It is easy to make and, as long as the temperature is around freezing, it won't melt.

TOOLS AND MATERIALS

- 2 containers, one smaller than the other
- Stones to weigh down the smaller container
- Pretty nature finds, such as colorful leaves and berries
- Scissors
- Pitcher
- Tea-light candle

1 You need two containers of a suitable size that will also fit in your freezer. I chose a plastic box that I usually use to store cookies and a paper coffee cup. My lantern is 8 inches in diameter and 3 inches tall. The "inside" cup is just large enough to accommodate a tea-light candle. You can make your lantern bigger or smaller, or in a different shape; you just need one container to be smaller than the other. A cake pan with a hole in the center is another option.

2 Place the smaller container in the center of the first. If you aren't planning to use the containers again, you can glue the small container to the bottom of the larger one to keep it in place. I wanted to reuse my containers, so I just weighed down the cup with a few stones. You need to glue or weigh down the smaller container, or it will float once you fill your masterpiece with water.

3 Now fill the large container with your nature finds. I used a branch of colorful leaves and berries I had found, but you can use anything you like. The ice will "preserve" whatever you use, so, if you plan ahead, you can even freeze summer flowers or wilted rose petals. Snip off sprigs of leaves and berries, then place in the large container, arranging them so they are facing outward, as this will create a nicer effect.

4 Use the pitcher to fill the large container with water, so all the nature finds are covered. You may find the tops stick out slightly, but that is fine as the water will expand when it freezes and cover them up. If you pour in more water, that is okay too, but you will have a slightly thicker layer of ice at the top and the finds will be most visible from the sides of the lantern.

5 Carefully transfer the lantern to the freezer. Keep in the freezer for a couple of days, so it is properly frozen throughout. Then remove the lantern from the freezer and leave it at room temperature to loosen up a bit, so you can easily take it out of the containers. The smaller container will probably be stuck to the ice, but don't panic—after 10 minutes or so you will be able to remove your lantern easily without any damage and add the tea-light candle.

I can imagine so many ways you could use this lantern to make an outdoor celebration that little bit more special, without having to buy anything at all. If you decide to create one of these lanterns in the middle of winter when there may be nothing at hand to collect, you can just make it with clear ice and it will still look magical with candlelight dancing inside.

CHAPTER

2

SPRING

LEAF POUNDING

Dyeing textiles with pigments from nature is one of the oldest coloring techniques. However, not everyone has the space and time to do this at home. Leaf or flower pounding is another way to get the natural pigments into the fabric. You can create beautiful home textiles, or even decorate T-shirts or tote bags. It is a great way to add color to older textiles or to reuse an item that has been stained beyond repair.

TOOLS AND MATERIALS

- Smooth cotton fabric
- Large bowl
- Unsweetened soy milk
- Leaves and flowers
- Masking tape
- Wooden chopping board
- Hammer
- Iron and ironing board
- Black textile marker

1 You need to pretreat the fabric first, so it will absorb the plant pigments. Whether the fabric is new or old, wash it in the washing machine on a long cycle. Do not use any laundry detergent or fabric softener, as you want to wash out as many chemicals as possible. Once that is done, soak the fabric in a large bowl in a solution of one part unsweetened soy milk and three parts water until it is thoroughly wet. Let soak overnight, and then air-dry.

2 Place the leaves and flowers facedown on the fabric in lines or mandalas, or in a random pattern. Use strips of masking tape to stick all the pieces to the fabric.

3 Gently lift the fabric and place it on top of the chopping board, with the taped leaves and flowers facing down. Carefully hammer over all the leaves and flowers to release their juices (and the pigments) into the fabric. You might want to use a piece of test fabric, as shown, to assess how hard you need to hammer to achieve the effect you want.

4 Let the pigments dry and set overnight, then peel off all the pieces of tape. Any odd bits of foliage or flowers that stick to the fabric can be easily scraped off with a fingernail.

5 Once you have removed all the tape, iron over the surface without steam to set the pigments into the fabric. I decided to give the whole piece a slightly more contemporary feel—and make it look just like a nature print—by drawing an outline around each leaf and flower with a black textile marker. Don't worry about drawing precise lines, as the design will look really artistic and cool if you simply outline the shapes and follow your imagination.

The colors on the fabric will fade slightly over time, but it will remain a beautiful piece that you will cherish. I use mine as a tablecloth, which makes every Sunday dinner special. You could also use the same technique to make place mats or other kitchen textiles, or to turn a bigger piece into a pair of drapes.

TIP

I recommend trying to hammer different types of leaves on the test fabric first, as not every leaf prints in the same way—usually, the softer the leaf, the easier it is to hammer the pigment out.

Egg Holder

TOOLS AND MATERIALS
- Soft, bendy twigs, such as birch or willow
- Hand pruners or sharp scissors

Easter always feels like the official start of spring, and bringing in some nature finds to celebrate feels so right. You can see the trees sprouting and fresh branches starting to appear—this is the best time to pick some twigs and make these tiny wreaths, which you can use for a long time afterward. Turn to the spring wreath (see page 48) and follow the same principles to create a teeny-tiny version to use as an egg holder for a tasty spring breakfast.

NATURE BRUSHES

TOOLS AND MATERIALS

- 3 twigs of comfortable thickness to hold
- Twine
- Nature finds such as fir, grass, and feathers
- Watercolor paints

One of the many fun projects that bring about surprising results are brushes made out of nature finds. Collect several twigs with a thickness that you find comfortable to hold and then use twine or tape to tie the brush material to the top. I tried different materials such as fir, grasses, and green blossoms. They work well if you use enough paint and want to create more of an abstract piece of art. These brushes are great fun for children too.

What was surprising—and something I will definitely use again—was a brush made out of feathers, which is more of an adult version. I collect feathers all the time, and for this brush I used three tiny feathers tied together. I was able to use the brush with watercolor and easily paint basic shapes such as this heart.

SPRING WREATH

Do you remember the winter wreath (see page 32)? This is the spring version, decorated with fresh greenery and flowers. I picked what was in the woods: lily-of-the-valley, blueberry branches, and some decorative grass.

TOOLS AND MATERIALS

- Soft, bendy twigs, such as birch or willow
- Spring greenery and flowers
- Hand pruners or sharp scissors
- Florist's wire or other craft wire

1 Start by creating the twig base. From my experience, birch and willow work really well because the twigs are long and bendy. Take a bunch of longer twigs, ideally one and a half times the length of the final circumference of the wreath, and twist them slightly, bending them around to form a circle.

2 Take a twig from those overlapping at the top and twist it around the wreath, tucking in the ends to hold them in place. Continue doing this with more of the twigs that overlap at the top until you have a neat and tidy wreath.

3 The quickest way to decorate the wreath is to create a number of tiny bunches of foliage and flowers of your choice. I created ten bunches. Divide the foliage and flowers into small bunches and cut them all to the same length. My wreath is about 8 inches in diameter, so I cut the bunches to a length of 4 inches. Use a length of wire to tie each bunch together, twisting it neatly around the stems to secure.

4 Start wherever you like, attaching a bunch to the wreath base with a length of wire—don't worry, the wire will not be visible for long.

5 All the bunches need to follow the same direction. After the first bunch is secured, position the second so that it covers the end of the first one—and also the wire fixing this to the wreath. Continue with the rest of your foliage and flower bunches. Once you've finished, check the wreath for any gaps and add some extra leaves to fill them.

Depending on the foliage and flowers you use, the wreath will last for a few days. Spraying the wreath with water or hanging it in a cooler place can make it last a bit longer. I hung this wreath on the door of my summerhouse, and it was an amazing spring decoration during my entire stay. Once the greenery dies, just cut out the bunches and keep the wreath base for decorating again the next week or the following season.

NATURE EGGS

Egg decorating is an Easter tradition in many countries, so here is a great project to show you how to do it in a more natural way. We all know that there are various methods for coloring eggs using ground-up herbs and leaves, but you can also use these materials in their raw state for decoration.

TOOLS AND MATERIALS
- Small, soft leaves
- Hollow eggs
- Craft glue
- Small paintbrush

1 Choose your leaves carefully. They need to be soft and thin for you to be able to glue them to the egg and also small enough so they can easily follow the egg's rounded shape. I decided to use only green leaves because flowers tend to lose or change their color.

2 Water down some craft glue. (If the glue is too thick, it will be really difficult to spread it over the leaves.) Once your glue is ready, dab a little on the shell, put the leaf in place, then cover the whole leaf with glue.

3 Repeat until you are happy with the leaf pattern. Don't worry about the white of the glue too much—once it dries, it will become transparent.

Repeat steps 1–3 to create a display of natural eggs using different leaves.

I was lucky enough to be able to source organic farm eggs in a range of different colors, which makes the final result even more beautiful. I chose random leaves I found in nature, ensuring they were the right size for the eggs. Clover turned out to be the most visually interesting and is my favorite, for sure.

BUTTERCUP CHANDELIER

My summerhouse in Sweden is surrounded by a sea of buttercups, so I want to share this very old Swedish craft, which uses these beautiful flowers. It's amazing what you can achieve with just a bunch of buttercups and your own hands.

TOOLS AND MATERIALS
- Spring flowers or grass
- Scissors
- Wooden clothespin or clip
- Natural twine

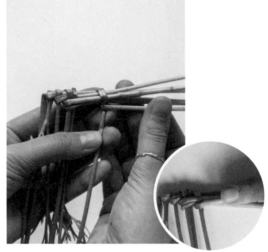

1 Choose flowers that have long (approximately 12 inches) but not woody stems, as they are less likely to break when bending. The number of stems you need will depend on the size of the chandelier you'd like to make, but I used about 50–60 for mine. If buttercups are not available where you are, this chandelier looks amazing made out of grass, too. Arrange the stems in a row with the flowers facing upward.

2 Pick one of the longest stems you have and bend it at right angles where you want the hanging part of the chandelier to start. Make sure that the flower is facing downward and the bent end to the right. This is the leading stem over which you will weave the other stems. Place the bent end of the leading stem over the row of flowers. Start with the stem closest to the leading stem and bend it over the bent end of that stem, so

the flower is facing downward. Then, take the tail end of the second stem under and over itself, and pull it to the right so that it is in line with the bent end of the leading stem. Push the loop you have created as close as possible to the leading stem. Repeat this process with all the flowers in the row, taking the bent end of each new stem under and over itself and all the preceding stems.

3 Continue in this way until the length of the braid is long enough to create the round shape of the chandelier. The beginning and end of the braid will need to overlap by about an inch for you to create the round shape, so, for the very last couple of loops, it is best to use thinner stems.

4 Once you have finished braiding, cut all the ends of the stems to the same length and then bring the end of the braid behind the beginning by about an inch, using the clothespin or clip to hold the circle in place.

5 Tie some twine firmly around the circle where the beginning and end of the braiding meet, and in another two or three places. Then tie all three or four pieces of twine together up high, so the chandelier can eventually be hung. Don't worry if all the flowers are not hanging down neatly and look as though they are sticking out. When they start drying, they will change and hang straighter.

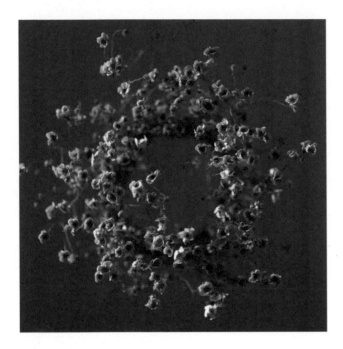

It was in this moment, when the sun hit the chandelier and brought out its buttery golden color, that I knew I just had to share this beautiful craft. Ideally, hang the chandelier in a spot where it will be protected from the elements to ensure that it dries beautifully. Alternatively, use the chandelier on the day you make it, perhaps to decorate a summer party or wedding.

With all the hard work that went into making the chandelier, however, I definitely wanted to keep mine for as long as possible. This particular one is a year old and, believe it or not, it does take that long for the flowers to completely lose their color. This beautiful decoration can hang in your home for many years, and will remind you of the sun on your face and the warmth of summer during those darker months.

CLAY PRINT

This simple craft is one of many easy ways in which you can preserve nature for a little longer. Once you have mastered the basic method, you can use it to create lots of different clay projects, from small hanging pieces to table decorations and coasters.

TOOLS AND MATERIALS
- Air-dry clay
- Rolling pin
- Cookie cutter, small glass, or rounded lid
- Foliage
- Toothpick (optional)
- Fine sandpaper
- Thick sewing thread (optional)

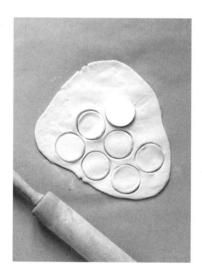

1 Roll the clay as you would cookie dough. The bigger the circles you want, the thicker the clay should be to ensure it won't crack. Use a little water to knead the clay first and make it nice and smooth. Cut out circles in the clay using a cookie cutter, small glass, or rounded lid. I chose a diameter of 2½–3 inches.

2 Select foliage that is about the same size as your clay disks. The best foliage for clay printing will have great textures, shapes, and patterns. Press the leaf into the clay with your fingers or roll over it gently with the rolling pin. Remove the leaf carefully.

3 To hang the disks, as I have here, create a hole in the top and bottom of each one with a toothpick, then let the clay dry. It usually takes about 24 hours for the clay to air-dry well, and I recommend you turn the pieces over about halfway through, which keeps the clay from bending too much. Once the disks are thoroughly dry, smooth the edges with some fine sandpaper. Then use some thick sewing thread to tie all the disks together.

I really love the imperfection of these clay disks. When you use the rolling pin to imprint the textures, the perfect clay circles get slightly deformed, following the shapes of nature, and that adds to the unique, handmade look. I photographed the finished products in a natural environment but, in reality, I have my decoration hanging at my kitchen window, which gets a lot of sun, highlighting the textures and shapes and casting the most beautiful shadows.

EGG PLANTER

TOOLS AND MATERIALS
- Empty shells
- Chive or watercress seeds
- Egg carton

Eggs are a popular breakfast, so this project is the perfect way to recycle the empty shells as tiny planters, which should serve you for a couple of weeks. You can plant simple herbs, such as chives or watercress, which grow super fast and will be ready to eat in a couple of days. Alternatively, you can use the shells as starter pots to sprout your spring vegetables and then "replant" the shells directly in the soil—they will serve as nutrition for the soil and so give back to nature.

FERN PRINT

Ferns are such magical plants. They flourish where nothing else is interested in growing, looking like they have been there for millions of years. They are not easy to work with, however, because they start curling almost right after you pick them from the ground, but they make such a wonderful stamp, so it is all worth it.

TOOLS AND MATERIALS
- Fern leaf
- Book for storing (optional)
- Nice paper or cardstock
- Black ink or paint
- Paintbrush
- Thin black marker pen (optional)

1 A little trick I've learned is to bring a book to the woods, then, once you find a leaf you like, you can put it between two pages right after you pick it to keep it nice and flat. To make the print, choose a piece of paper or cardstock that's a bit bigger than your leaf. I recommend not using paper that is too structured, as the print won't stick as easily.

2 To make it easier to cover the leaf, the medium you use needs to be quite watery. I recommend using ink, watered-down acrylic, or watercolor paint. Paint one side of the leaf and when it is completely covered, turn it over and stamp it on the paper or cardstock. Press on the leaf with your fingers to ensure the whole leaf print is transferred to the paper.

3 You can use the same leaf to stamp two or three prints. The first print will be very saturated and the next lighter, but still as beautiful. The prints will never be perfect—this is nature, after all—and every leaf is unique, so don't worry too much about "imperfect" prints. To add a bit more detail, you can always take a thin black marker pen and draw in the outlines or any missing pieces.

These fern prints work as beautiful decorations for your walls—you can frame them or simply tape them straight onto the wall—or as birthday and greeting cards. Feel free to experiment with different colors and papers, too.

FEATHER BOUQUET

TOOLS AND MATERIALS
- Branches or twigs
- Feathers
- Vase
- Thin florist's wire or other craft wire

A traditional Norwegian thing to do around spring and Easter time is to make a display of feathers. Simply collect a few branches or twigs and some feathers. Then cut the twigs down so they will fit inside a vase and start decorating them with the feathers. Smaller feathers are best, but if you do this with kids, then bigger ones might be easier. Use small pieces of thin wire to fasten the feathers to the ends of the twigs one by one. I used about a dozen feathers for the display shown here. This is another beautiful bouquet that will not die any time soon and can be used to decorate your home throughout spring.

TINY TERRARIUM

I love plants and have too many of them at home. What I enjoy even more is bringing plants and nature finds home. With this tiny terrarium you can do just that. Over time, the jar will become its own little forest full of roots and beautiful green moss.

TOOLS AND MATERIALS
- Empty glass jar
- Pebbles and sea glass
- Soil or potting mix
- Small plant shoot
- Fresh moss
- Small plastic animals or pretty stones

1 The jar can be any size you like, but it will be helpful if you can fit your hand inside easily to arrange everything. Wash the jar thoroughly in hot, soapy water, and then rinse well. Start filling the jar with a layer of pebbles. I also added some sea glass for contrast.

2 The next layer consists of soil or potting mix and whatever plant you wish to grow in your tiny ecosystem. I found this small maple shoot in the woods, but you could use a shoot from any small houseplant you have at home, as long as it likes a moister environment. Place the shoot in the jar, sprinkling in a little more soil or potting mix to help keep it upright.

3 The last step is to decorate the surface. Carefully spread and place pieces of fresh moss, as well as some decorative elements, on the soil or potting mix. For example, if you are making the terrarium for children, you could create a dinosaur park or farm with some small dinosaur or animal figures. I decided to use some pretty stones I found in the mountains and a few I collected on my travels.

NATURE DISPLAY

A great way to bring nature indoors is to frame it. You can use a regular picture frame with a solid back, but I love how the light goes through the double-glass panel of this frame, as it highlights all the shades of green. You don't need to buy a fancy picture frame either—I just bought two of the same cheap frames and replaced the back of one with the glass of the other.

Collect whatever prettily shaped leaves and flowers you find, arrange them over one of the glass panels, and then cover them with the other. Be careful to pick the leaves and flowers on a dry day so you can enjoy the display for as long as possible.

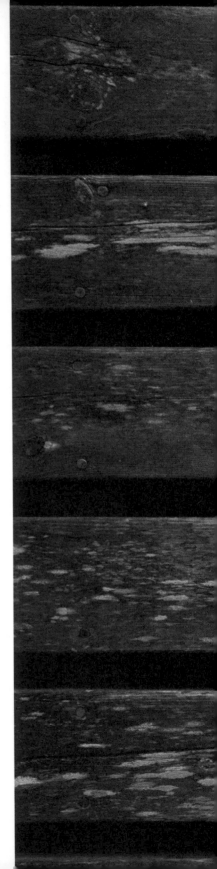

SEED BALLS

If you live in a city as I do, you might see ugly patches of land around every corner. Have you ever dreamed of looking at beautiful flowers there instead of weeds and soil? I created these seed balls for that very reason—it's also a lot of fun to walk around town and indulge in a bit of guerrilla gardening. You simply toss the seed balls—or seed bombs as they are sometimes known—onto patches of bare soil and let nature take its course.

TOOLS AND MATERIALS
- Wildflower seeds, preferably from local plants
- Potting mix
- All-purpose flour
- Mixing bowl
- Tablespoon

1 You need to prepare or collect your seeds first. Either buy them from a store or ask a friend with a garden to share some with you. Or you can collect them from the wild yourself. I used a lot of poppy seeds, which are super easy to collect at the end of the season, as well as various wildflower seeds local to my area. It is better to use smaller seeds; otherwise the balls will fall apart easily once dry.

2 Mix some potting mix with the flour. The amounts you need will depend on the number of seed balls you want to make, but for seven balls I used about five tablespoons of potting mix and one tablespoon of flour. Stir the potting mix and flour together until they are evenly mixed—as if you were mixing the ingredients for a cake.

3 Next, mix in the seeds, again mixing them in properly as if you were baking a cake, so they are distributed evenly through the mixture.

4 Add enough water to make a "dough." You need very little water as the seeds will start to sprout if the mixture is too moist. I used about one tablespoon of water, but the amount will depend on how moist your potting mix is to begin with. Start with one tablespoon and mix it in well; if you have a thick dough, that is enough water. The mixture needs to be just moist enough to hold together—the water and flour will work together like a natural glue.

5 To form a seed ball, take about a spoonful of the mixture and mold it gently into an even ball with your fingers and thumbs. If you want to make the process even easier, or if you are working with children, you can use an ice-cube tray and just press the mixture into the individual compartments. Once you have finished molding the balls, let them dry and then you are ready to go.

Seed balls also make a great gift for all garden and flower lovers. They look a little like delicious truffles, so you could present them nicely in a small gift box or paper bag and give them away to friends, family, or even your child's teachers.

Alternatively, carry the seed balls in your pocket when you go out for a walk. Then, when you see a patch of ground that deserves a bit of love, just throw a seed ball and come back in a couple of weeks to see the flowers in bloom.

3

SUMMER

FLOWER PRESSING

Drying flowers is a great way to preserve and enjoy beautiful petals the whole year round. There is a bit of magic involved, too, as you never quite know what the outcome will be—some flowers will keep their color perfectly, whereas others will fade. Apart from a little patience, you don't need anything special to complete this project, so get ready to preserve countless memories from summer walks.

TOOLS AND MATERIALS
- Flowers and leaves
- Paper towels
- Thick, heavy books
- Tweezers (optional)
- Wax paper

1 To ensure the flowers don't go moldy, you should always pick them on a dry, sunny day. If you can, start pressing the flowers as soon as possible—take a book and rubber band with you on walks and begin the process there and then.

2 Place a paper towel over two pages of a thick book. Fold the paper towel in half, then open it out again. The paper towel will protect the pages of the book. Arrange the flowers over the right-hand half of the paper towel, giving them enough room to expand as they flatten.

3 Feel free to press gently on the flowers with your fingers to keep them in the position you want. You may need to remove some leaves or even petals to make the flowers lie nice and flat.

4 Repeat steps 2 and 3, leaving at least 30 pages between each of the pressing pages. Once all your flowers are in place, close the book and put it somewhere safe. Weigh it down with a couple of heavy books. If you wish, you can add to the weight with a heavy plant pot. What you use should not be too heavy, however, or you risk damaging the flowers. Leave the book for a week or two without opening it.

5 After a week or two, carefully open the book and transfer the half-dried flowers from the paper towels to some folded wax paper. You may need to use tweezers to do this. Wait two more weeks and your flowers will be dried and ready for your next craft project.

I have never been a huge fan of dried-flower bouquets and similar decorations. But I think pressing flowers is something different; it is almost as if you are turning the beautiful textures and shapes of nature into a living drawing. After four weeks most of the dried flowers will still keep their color, almost as vivid as when they were alive, and you can use them for a number of different craft projects—I show you my favorite ones in this book. If you decide to dry the flowers just to preserve them, then opening your book full of spring and summer treasures in the middle of a dark winter will be most satisfying.

PRINTING WITH SHELLS

You can create unique textile designs by using textured shells as stamps. Decorate anything, from home textiles to clothes, and print with one or more colors in an organized or a random pattern. I decided to combine red and shades of pink, which are my favorite colors. You can use the same shell for different colors, creating one harmonious pattern, or use different shells for more variety.

TOOLS AND MATERIALS
- Plain fabric
- Shell with a good texture
- Paper
- Textile paints and paintbrush
- Detergent

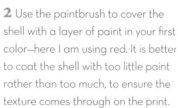

1 If your fabric is brand new, wash it a couple of times to get rid of any chemicals and to ensure the paint will stick to it. It is best to choose a plain fabric with no texture so you can control the print and get nice detailed shapes. Place the shell on a piece of paper to protect your work surface when painting.

2 Use the paintbrush to cover the shell with a layer of paint in your first color—here I am using red. It is better to coat the shell with too little paint rather than too much, to ensure the texture comes through on the print.

3 For the best results, keep the shell on your work surface with the painted side facing up and press the fabric onto it. Use your fingers to press the fabric into all the grooves. Paint the shell again after each print. If you feel the paint is getting too smudgy, wash the shell in hot, soapy water and start over. Repeat with the different colors until you achieve the desired effect.

FLORAL GARLAND

TOOLS AND MATERIALS
- Bunches of white flowers
- Linen twine
- Clothespins

My love for decorating with nature is never-ending. It is affordable, easily accessible, and planet-friendly. This floral garland can be made big, bold, and bright or simple and down-to-earth—either way, it is very easy to make.

For this garland, which is great for parties, weddings, or just a fancy Sunday lunch, I only used white flowers with yellow centers, to create a cottage-garden, countryside effect and give it a feeling of simplicity. I strung some nice linen twine across the room and then used clothespins to clip tiny bunches of flowers to it. That way, it is easy to put up and take down the garland. If you decide to keep the garland for longer, the flowers will dry in this position and can decorate your room for weeks.

DREAMCATCHER

I love birds and collecting different feathers, but I never really know what to do with them. So, I created this simple dreamcatcher to put the feathers to good use. You can really personalize this project to suit your taste and style by using colored twine, painting the branches in different colors, or adding colorful beads, for example.

TOOLS AND MATERIALS

- 3 twigs of the same length and thickness
- Craft knife (optional)
- Crystals and beads
- Feathers
- Twine
- Scissors
- Electric drill
- Craft glue

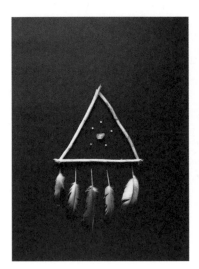  

1 It is a good idea to collect and prepare everything, and plan your dreamcatcher first. You will need three twigs of the same length and thickness to create a base triangle. I whittled mine down with a craft knife and got rid of the bark to make the twigs lighter. Then decide where you would like your feathers and other decorations to go.

2 Once you are happy with your design, arrange the twigs in a triangle. Tie the three corners of the triangle together with twine, leaving the ends long and loose. Ensure the twine is secure, as it is important to tighten the frame properly.

3 To create the center netting, I used a crystal with a hole drilled through the middle, but you can use any stone or bead that you like. Thread three pieces of twine through the middle of the crystal, knotted at one end to hold them in place, then pull tight and tie one thread to each corner of the triangle.

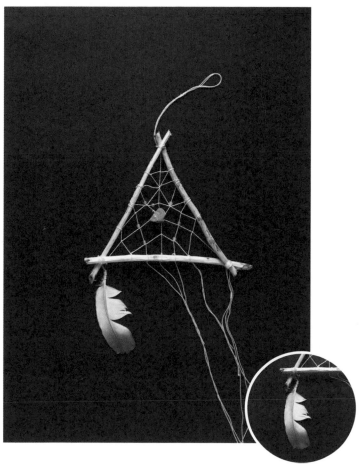

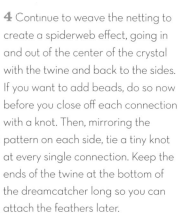

4 Continue to weave the netting to create a spiderweb effect, going in and out of the center of the crystal with the twine and back to the sides. If you want to add beads, do so now before you close off each connection with a knot. Then, mirroring the pattern on each side, tie a tiny knot at every single connection. Keep the ends of the twine at the bottom of the dreamcatcher long so you can attach the feathers later.

5 Starting at one corner of the triangle, tie the feathers to the dreamcatcher one by one. The ends of feathers tend to be slippery, so you can either tie the twine directly to each feather or use a little glue to stick the twine in place. Once you are finished, tie the loose end of each length of twine firmly around the bottom twig and cut off any excess.

Even if you don't believe in the magical powers of dreamcatchers, they are an attractive decoration. If you use things that you have found in nature, then they are also a lovely reminder of a beautiful day outdoors. I have my dreamcatcher hanging from a window frame, so the feathers start dancing when the wind blows.

TWIG HEART

A twig heart is a great project to make at the end of summer. Not only is it super easy to create, but you can scale it up or down and decorate it however you like. It looks amazing by itself, but I added a couple of decorative grasses that I collected over the summer to give it more oomph. Hang the finished heart on a door or wall for decoration.

TOOLS AND MATERIALS
- Bendy twigs, such as birch or willow
- Florist's wire or other craft wire
- Scissors
- Decorative grasses

1 You need really bendy twigs, so collect them just before you decide to make the heart, or leave them in a vase of water to keep fresh until you're ready. I used birch, as that is easy to get hold of where I live, but willow is great, too. Divide the twigs into two bunches. Braid the bunches together at one end, and then secure with a length of wire.

2 Take the long ends of the twigs and bend them slowly down toward you, creating a heart shape as you do so. You may find this a bit difficult at first, but you'll soon get the hang of it. Once you are happy with the shape and size of the heart, fix the twigs in position with more wire in the same place that you secured the ends. Cut away the leftover ends.

3 If you decide to decorate your heart with grasses, make two small bunches and fix them to the bottom with a length of wire. Once this is done, play around with the grass stems a bit and spread them out evenly to fill the heart shape.

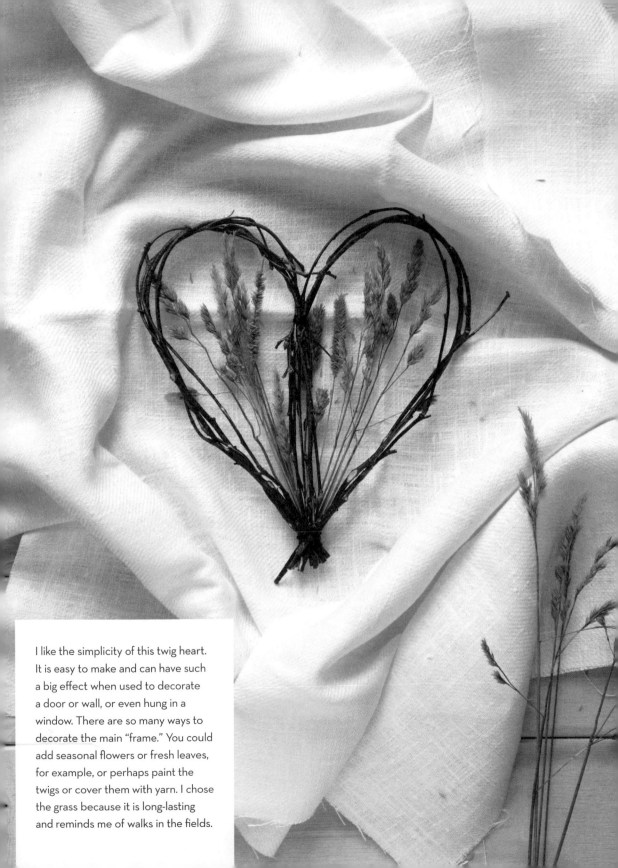

I like the simplicity of this twig heart. It is easy to make and can have such a big effect when used to decorate a door or wall, or even hung in a window. There are so many ways to decorate the main "frame." You could add seasonal flowers or fresh leaves, for example, or perhaps paint the twigs or cover them with yarn. I chose the grass because it is long-lasting and reminds me of walks in the fields.

PRESSED FLOWERS CANDLE

You can easily make this decorative candle from items you have lying around at home. Choose flowers that match the color scheme in your home for the perfect table centerpiece or give the candle as a gift, picking the recipient's favorite flowers as the floral feature. I explain how to press and dry flowers in the flower pressing project on page 76.

TOOLS AND MATERIALS

- Glass jar
- Dried flowers and leaves
- Scissors
- Craft glue and paintbrush
- Old candle wax or wax pellets
- Heatproof container and saucepan
- Oven mitt
- Candlewick
- Wooden clothespin

1 Wash the jar thoroughly. Pick and prepare your dried flowers and trim them down to fit inside the jar. You can use whole flowers, leaves, or petals. Bigger flowers can be more difficult to bend to the shape of the jar, so smaller, thinner blooms or petals are best. Press the flower, leaf, or petal against the inside of the jar and paint with glue to make it stick. Repeat for all of your dried material, then leave to dry thoroughly.

2 To prepare the wax, you need to create a water bath in the same way that you would melt chocolate. Use wax scrapings from old candles or some wax pellets, which you can buy in all good craft stores. Melt the wax in a heatproof container placed in a saucepan of boiling water.

3 Once the wax has melted, pour it slowly and carefully into the jar, protecting your hands with an oven mitt. Place the candlewick in the center of the jar and use a wooden peg balanced on the rim to hold it in place while the wax solidifies.

FOREVER BOUQUET

TOOLS AND MATERIALS
- Pressed flowers and leaves
- Black craft paper
- Craft glue, such as PVA
  (colorless when dry)

When I looked at all the dried flowers I collected for the flower pressing project (see page 76), they immediately reminded me of beautiful still-life paintings. So, I decided to arrange more dried flowers into a bouquet and frame it on a black paper background to simulate a painting.

Use your imagination and create a bouquet you like by arranging flowers and leaves in different displays. Think in terms of layers: arrange the back layer of bigger blossoms and greenery, then add a layer of smaller flowers on top, to create the illusion of a bouquet. You can cut the flowers from the stems and leaves to make them easier to arrange, and add the greenery separately.

Shell Wall Hanging

TOOLS AND MATERIALS

- Long, thick branch
- Seashells
- Craft glue
- Twine

A wall hanging made with beautiful shells collected at the beach will remind you of an amazing summer vacation all year round. I used a gorgeous branch that I found in the woods and added a bit of color in the form of sea snails with closed and open shells.

Decide how you want to arrange your shells, drip a couple of drops of craft glue into each one, then stick the end of some twine inside. I sorted my shells by size and created an arrow shape by placing the biggest shell in the middle and making the twine shorter as it traveled outward. Once you are happy with your arrangement, tie all the loose ends of twine together at the top, loop each piece of twine and its shell around the branch once to hold it in place, and hang the piece on the wall ready to be admired.

FLOWER CROWN

- Twig wreath base
- Fresh summer flowers
- Hand pruners or sharp scissors
- Florist's wire or other craft wire

Do you remember the wreath we made in spring (see page 48)? I kept the frame because you can decorate it over and over again throughout the year with different nature finds. This time, I chose some late-summer flowers and made a summer crown. This would look beautiful hanging as a wreath, as well as adorning your head at a summer garden party.

Floral crowns are a big tradition in Scandinavia, especially in Sweden for midsummer, where making a crown is one of the skills that many girls learn. You follow the same technique as for the spring wreath, but use mostly flowers and as little green as possible. Here, I decided to cover only half of the twig frame, which is another option when creating a wreath as it enables you to showcase both the flowers and the frame.

SHELL CANDLES

TOOLS AND MATERIALS
- Oyster shells
- Old candle wax or wax pellets
- Heatproof container and saucepan
- Oven mitt
- Candlewick

The larger shells from oysters and other shellfish are just like tiny bowls, so creating tea-light candles with them is a great way to reuse treasures collected on vacations by the sea. That way, you don't keep the beautiful shells hidden away, but can use them as a decoration for summer parties or perhaps a fancy dinner. The other great thing about these candles is that you only need a small amount of wax to fill the shells and can split one wick into several smaller ones to create a whole set. If you wish, you can just melt away the wax from a basic tea-light candle and even use the wick exactly as it is since it's the perfect size for a shell.

Melt some candle wax in a water bath (see page 90) and then pour the wax into the dry, empty shells. You might need to support the shells to keep them level as you do this. Since the shells are very shallow, the wax will solidify quickly, so just hold each wick in place for a few minutes and then the candles are ready for lighting.

PRESSED FLOWERS CARD

One of the many ways to use your dried flowers and leaves is to create unique cards, which are great for birthdays, wedding invitations, and much more. Feel free to use paper in different colors—you can even use the pages from old books. I explain how to press/dry flowers in the flower pressing project on page 76.

TOOLS AND MATERIALS

- Dried flowers
- Scissors
- Plain greeting card
- Craft glue and paintbrush
- Embroidery floss and needle
- Pen

1 Pick and prepare your dried flowers. Cut the flowers to fit the card, then arrange them to get the look you want—you can create a pattern, spread them randomly, or create a tiny posy as I did. Once you're happy with the floral design, add a tiny bit of glue to the card, place the flowers on top, and glue over everything. Once the glue has dried, you won't be able to see it.

2 To decorate the card and add a little more texture, make a little ribbon to tie the posy together using embroidery floss and a needle. Stitch the floss through the card and then tie the ends into a small bow.

3 Depending on the occasion, you might want to add a little personal note, name, greeting, or so on to finish off your card. Here, I used a black pen to add a simple handwritten note.

PEBBLE GAME

One of my favorite activities is collecting different pebbles and stones. They are a wonderful creative material when it comes to making board games. The great thing is that you don't need much to turn a few pebbles into a crisscross or simple chess game. You can create the game then and there while you are out in nature, using a marker to draw on the pebbles and whatever you have on hand as a board—be it a newspaper, wrapping paper, or a piece of cloth.

If you want to put a bit more effort into it and create a gift or a lasting memory from a vacation, then you can use a piece of leftover linen fabric to create a "chessboard" by painting it with black and white acrylic paint. To make the work with the pebbles a little easier, I drew simple sketches of the chess symbols on them in pencil first, then colored them with black and white paint. What is ingenious about this textile "board" is that you can turn it into a little pouch tied with a piece of ribbon to create a travel version of the game.

TOOLS AND MATERIALS
- Flat pebbles of two different shades
- Pencil and paintbrush
- Black and white acrylic paint
- Large square of linen fabric

FLORAL LAMPSHADE

This is one of my favorite projects in the whole book. Although it takes a bit more effort to create, the result is a unique and long-lasting home decoration. Reuse and recycle an old lampshade, give it new life, and capture the memories of summer when you turn it on during long winter nights. I explain how to press/dry flowers in the flower pressing project on page 76.

TOOLS AND MATERIALS

- Old lampshade with a metal frame
- Baking/tracing paper
- Pencil
- Scissors
- Sewing pins or tape
- White iron-on interfacing (one-sided)
- Dried flowers
- Tweezers (optional)
- Piece of old cloth
- Iron and ironing board
- Hot-glue gun or textile glue

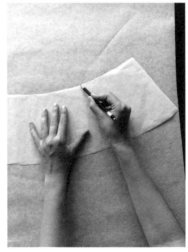

The less angled the lampshade, the easier you will find it to work with. If you can, look for one that is as close as possible to a cylindrical shape.

1 Remove the old fabric from the lampshade first and then create a template for the new lampshade out of baking/tracing paper. Cut a piece of paper big enough to go around the whole frame and connect it at either end with a sewing pin or a piece of tape. Cut off the excess, leaving ¼ inch at the top and bottom that can be glued to the frame later.

2 Remove the template from the frame and use it to cut out two mirrored pieces from the interfacing. To do this, place the interfacing, with the unglued side facing up, on a flat surface. Put the template on top and draw around it. Flip the template over and trace another outline on the interfacing. Cut out both outlines.

3 Place one piece of interfacing on a flat surface, with the glue side facing up. Choose your dried flowers and arrange them as you wish over the interfacing—you might need to use tweezers for precision—ensuring there is a gap of ¼ inch between the flowers and the top and bottom of the interfacing. Keep in mind that the lampshade is rounded and angled, so the flowers should follow its shape.

4 Put some old cloth on the ironing board to protect it, then carefully place your composition on top. Put the second piece of interfacing, glue side facing down, on top of the first, so that both glue sides are touching. Iron slowly, without using any steam.

5 Check that the flowers are facing outward, then wrap the interfacing around the frame, leaving an excess of ¼ inch at both the top and bottom. Pin the interfacing in place. Starting on one side and working your way around, fold the excess interfacing over the top and under the bottom of the frame. Remove the pins and glue the ends of the interfacing together to secure, then glue the excess to the top and bottom of the frame.

If you wish, you can decorate the lampshade with some lace or tassels, but I really like the simplicity of it as it is, because it allows the flowers to shine. I used mainly flowers that were interesting in shape and darker in color, to ensure they would create a nice contrast once the lamp was switched on. I loved the lampshade so much that I made another one using only yellow flowers, and it worked just as well.

Over the years, the flowers turn brown and the fabric takes on a vintage yellow tint, but the lampshade will still look like a piece of art for many years to come.

Note: If you have a tiny lampshade and the light bulb will be very close to it, make sure to use an LED bulb.

CHAPTER

4

FALL

Acorn Mushrooms

Oak leaves and acorns are two of my favorite things in nature. The shapes are just so beautiful. Don't the acorns look like mushrooms with those tiny hats? So, for this project, that's what I did—I turned acorns into little decorative mushrooms and fungi.

For the brown boletus I used a whole acorn. Paint the hat brown and the body a light pink-brown with some darker brown shading. For the mushroom to stand up, you need to turn the body upside down, so the flat top works as a foot, then glue the hat on top.

For the toadstool, paint the hats red with white dots. As these mushrooms have a more sleek, slim look, white air-dry clay is best for creating the stems. Play around with the heights of the mushrooms and make each one slightly different.

It was great fun creating this tiny woodland scene, and with a bit of moss, you can make a festive table setting.

TOOLS AND MATERIALS
- Acorns
- Acrylic paints and paintbrush
- Craft glue
- White air-dry clay

week 41

DRAWING ON LEAVES

TOOLS AND MATERIALS

- Large leaves
- Thick, heavy book for pressing (optional)
- Acrylic paints and paintbrush or marker pens

Simple, boring leaves can be transformed into placement cards for a dinner party or perhaps a personalized gift tag. Depending on the shape or color of the leaf you choose, you can create a unique piece of art.

Pick bigger leaves with a smooth surface, so you have space to write and draw. Then dry the leaves out flat between the pages of a book or, to give them more texture, let them dry naturally and enjoy how the edges curl.

Once the leaves are dry, have fun drawing and writing with some acrylic paint or an all-surface marker pen.

ROWAN HEARTS

TOOLS AND MATERIALS
- Rowan berries
- Florist's wire or other craft wire

I absolutely love that time of year when fall is on the way and bright red rowan berries start popping up everywhere. In Scandinavia, it is traditional to string rowan berries onto some linen thread and then hang this from the rail of a drape. I wanted to take this idea a step further, and this is the result.

You will need some florist's wire or other craft wire that is firm enough to poke through the berries. Thread the berries onto the wire, bend the wire into a heart shape, and twist the wire at the ends to close the shape. Make as many hearts as you wish. I suspended mine from some twiggy stems.

The berries will dry out after a while, leaving tiny gaps in between. The great thing is that once the berries are dry, you can keep the garlands for a long time and perhaps use them to decorate a Christmas tree later in the winter.

APPLE GARLAND

TOOLS AND MATERIALS

- Apples
- Kitchen knife, grater, or mandoline
- Water and lemon juice in a bowl
- Dish towel
- Cooling rack
- Needle and twine

Preserving apples by drying them is simple to do and allows you to create a delicious treat for cold days as well as a great kitchen decoration.

The key to well-dried apples is to cut them into equal, or similarly sized, slices. You can slice the apples with a knife, grater, or mandoline. First, prepare a bowl of water and lemon juice in a ratio of 8:1 to prevent the apple slices from going brown. Cut the apples in half horizontally and remove the seeds. Then cut them into slices a few millimeters thick. Pop each slice in the bowl of lemon water.

You can dry your apples in a commercial fruit dryer or place them on a dish towel on top of your radiator. Alternatively, pop them in the microwave on high power for three minutes or until the edges begin to curl. Flip the apple slices and microwave for another minute. Leave to cool on a rack until crisp.

Once the slices are ready, thread them onto a long piece of natural twine. You might find it easier to do this by threading the twine onto a large needle first and pushing this through the center of each slice. Display the garland in the kitchen, hanging it from a shelf as an easily available snack in the fall.

HALLOWEEN MASK

TOOLS AND MATERIALS

- Large fall leaves, such as maple leaves
- Thick, heavy book
- Sharp craft knife
- Acrylic paints and paintbrush or marker pens

Need a quick fix to make several masks for a children's party? With the fall comes a lot of wonderful natural material that is available right outside your door. Pick the biggest leaves you can find and get creative. I used maple leaves because they are easy to spot and also big enough to cover an adult face.

If the leaves are curling up a bit, place them between the pages of a large, heavy book for a while to flatten them. Then, using a very sharp craft knife, cut out two holes for the eyes. Be careful to cut slowly so you don't tear the leaf.

Now the fun starts. You can use different marker pens or acrylic paints and a paintbrush to decorate the leaf and create an animal mask straight out of your imagination. Due to their color and shape, maple leaves lend themselves especially well to the face of a fox, cat, or lion. But let your imagination run wild and use your leaf as a blank canvas to create a natural Halloween mask.

LEAF MOBILE

I love decorating with nature finds because it is easy and affordable, and also lets you bring a bit of the beauty from outside into your home.

To create this leaf mobile, you can use the leaves from the preserving leaves project (see page 128) and the twiggy base from the spring wreath (see page 48) as a supporting frame. Or, you could hang your leaves from a circular or square picture frame. Here, I used an embroidery hoop that I had at home.

Tie three strings of the same length to your choice of supporting frame and tie the other ends together. Cut several more pieces of string for hanging the decorations. I opted for thin linen twine, but you could also use embroidery floss, thread, or even some fishing line if you want to keep the hangings invisible. Then attach your decorations. I chose preserved leaves, but feel free to use whatever you find in nature—I also used some small, brightly colored felt mushrooms.

I started by hanging bigger leaves at the same height, spacing them out evenly to create a "floor" of leaves. I then filled the gaps with a few smaller leaves, but hung them slightly higher. Once you have hung all the leaves, the mobile is finished, or you can continue decorating with fall berries or other decorations, depending on your preference.

As the leaves are preserved, they won't change their shape or color very much, so you can enjoy the mobile as a permanent decoration—in a woodland-themed children's room, for example.

TOOLS AND MATERIALS

- Preserved leaves or other nature finds
- Small decorations
- Twig wreath base, picture frame, or embroidery hoop
- String or fishing line
- Scissors

SIMPLE FALL WREATH

TOOLS AND MATERIALS

• Long branches of vine leaves
• Florist's wire or other
  craft wire

The colors of fall leaves are so impressive that you can create
something very simple that still has a big impact. These striking
vine leaves are a perfect example, usually having the brightest
red, orange, and almost pinkish shades. What is also great about
vine leaves is that they basically grow everywhere, and no one
will mind you taking a branch or two as they will grow back
quickly next spring. The branches are also very soft and bendy,
which makes them easy to work with.

It only takes about five minutes to create this simple yet effective
wreath. Collect a few longer branches of vine leaves and bend
them into a circle. You won't be able to create a very big wreath
without support, so I recommend going no bigger than the size
of a dining plate. Continue making the circle, wrapping your
branches around and around. You might have to secure some of
the branches with a piece of florist's wire. Continue with a second
and third layer of branches, turning and twisting them to fill the
empty spaces between the leaves and create a neat, even look.

NATURE CONFETTI

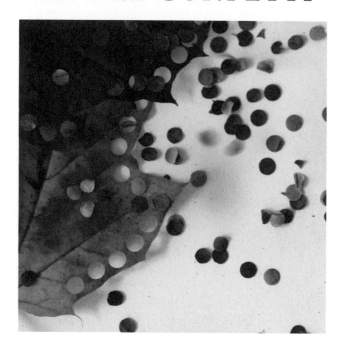

TOOLS AND MATERIALS
- Colorful fall leaves
- Hole puncher

Parties and celebrations tend not to be the most nature-friendly gatherings, often because people use environmentally unfriendly confetti. With this natural confetti, however, you can be a bit more eco-friendly while still having a great party. It is also so easy to make. Just collect some leaves in pretty colors, preferably those that feel "leathery" as they are firmer and much easier to work with. Then use a regular office hole puncher and punch through the leaves to create colorful natural confetti.

The great thing about this confetti is that once it dries out, you can more or less use it forever, at any time. It is also even better to throw than other types of confetti because the dried leaves almost feel and sound like rustling paper. The confetti will lose its color over time and get darker, but you can still enjoy it for many weeks regardless.

LEAFY CROWN

Creating a crown out of leaves is another great way to dress up for Halloween without using plastic. You can use lots of different colorful leaves to make a variety of striking crowns.

TOOLS AND MATERIALS
- White craft paper or cardstock
- Scissors
- Colorful fall leaves
- Needle and thread

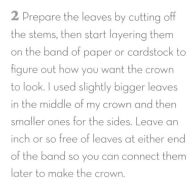

1 To make the headband for the crown, cut a strip of craft paper or cardstock, 1¼–1½ inches wide, and make sure it is long enough to go around your head with a bit left over to connect the ends later. The width of the paper or cardstock you need will depend on the leaves you are using, as you don't want the band of the crown to show through.

2 Prepare the leaves by cutting off the stems, then start layering them on the band of paper or cardstock to figure out how you want the crown to look. I used slightly bigger leaves in the middle of my crown and then smaller ones for the sides. Leave an inch or so free of leaves at either end of the band so you can connect them later to make the crown.

3 Once you have decided on a pattern, position the first leaf, bend the bottom under the band, and, using a needle and thread, stitch neatly in place. I chose yellow thread because it makes the stitching almost invisible. Repeat until all the leaves are stitched to your crown.

Note: To close the crown, overlap the ends of the band and sew one last leaf over them to hide the join.

PRESERVING LEAVES

Collecting leaves of all colors is one of my favorite activities, but I soon realized that they lose their bright colors very quickly. You can enjoy their beauty a little longer by preserving them in beeswax to create a long-lasting decorative material that can be incorporated into your next craft project. I love working with beeswax as it is natural, smells amazing, and keeps the warmth of the leaves' colors by giving them a slightly yellow coating.

TOOLS AND MATERIALS
- Fresh, colorful fall leaves
- Beeswax and heatproof old glass or small pitcher
- Saucepan and oven mitt
- Scrap paper
- 2 wooden sticks, twine or string, and 2 plant pots, or any type of small drying rack
- Clothespins

1 Collect the leaves and preserve them as soon as you can. Once leaves fall from a tree, they start losing their pigment, so the fresher they are when preserved, the better. Prepare everything for the project before you go for your walk, so you can get started as soon as you get home. Clean or dry the leaves if there is any dirt or water on them.

2 Melt the beeswax in a water bath (see page 90). Make sure to melt the wax in a glass or pitcher that's big enough for you to dip the leaf in and out easily. Once the wax has melted, dip each leaf in quickly and then carefully shake off the excess. Place each dipped leaf on some scrap paper. The wax cools quite quickly, which can result in too thick a layer of wax on the leaves, so you'll need to keep reheating it.

3 Once you have dipped the leaves, you need to hang them up to dry. I created a small drying station on my desk by sticking two wooden sticks tied with string into a couple of plant pots. Put some scrap paper underneath the leaves to protect your work surface. Clip each leaf to the string with a clothespin and let dry thoroughly. The leaves will only take a couple of minutes to dry. They might curl under the weight of the wax, but you can gently bend them back into shape.

These colorful leaves are wonderful for creating guessing games if you preserve lots of different types. They can also be used to decorate festive dinners or parties, or just a room for every day—and I love that they make a room smell slightly of honey.

GREAT FOR KIDS

LEAF ROSES

People say that fall is the season when every leaf becomes a flower, so why not create a flower out of colorful leaves? These roses are easy to make once you get the hang of it. You can either make a single rose as a decoration or a whole bouquet to give to someone as a gift. Maple leaves are especially beautiful, as they make deep red roses. And, once the leaves dry out, the roses look almost like real dried ones.

TOOLS AND MATERIALS

- Colorful fall leaves
- Wooden barbecue sticks
- Paper sticky tape
- Scissors
- Dark green acrylic paint and paintbrush
- Cardboard

1 Collect and prepare your leaves. I used eight maple leaves for one rose. Make sure the leaves are fresh because they break more easily if they are dry. Remove all the stems.

2 Take a barbecue stick and start creating the rose from the center. Fold the first leaf in half horizontally and then roll it around the stick—roll very tightly at the beginning and then a little looser. Keep folding and rolling at least three leaves to create the rosebud in the center.

3 Once you are happy with the rosebud, pick smaller leaves—or tear bigger leaves into smaller, petal-size pieces—and arrange them around the bud, molding and holding them in place with your fingers. Repeat this step a couple of times until you are pleased with the result.

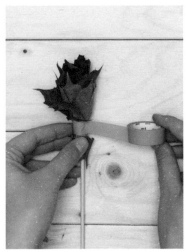

4 To finish the rose, use your thumb and fingers to squeeze the leaves together tightly at the bottom and then wind some tape around a couple of times to keep them in position on the stick. If you wish, you can also tape a leaf farther down the stick.

5 Once all the leaves are taped neatly in place and you are happy with your creation, paint over the tape and stick with dark green paint to create an even more realistic-looking stem. Stick the finished rose in a piece of cardboard until it has dried out completely.

I really enjoy the variety of roses you can make in this way. You can keep some roses tiny to give the impression of rosebuds, and make some very open and fully bloomed. Why not create a bouquet that you can put in a vase as a lovely fall decoration?

LEAF-SHAPED TRINKET DISH

Leaves not only have wonderful colors but also interesting shapes and textures. Imprinting a leaf in air-dry clay allows you to preserve the shape and texture, and then use the clay to create something practical, such as a trinket dish for jewelry or perhaps storing hairpins or keys.

TOOLS AND MATERIALS
- Air-dry clay
- Rolling pin
- Leaf with visible structure
- Sharp knife
- Small bowl and baking paper
- Spray paint or watercolor paints and paintbrush
- Clear lacquer spray

1 Roll out the clay. To make a palm-sized dish, I recommend rolling out the clay until it is about ¼ inch thick. That way, you can be sure the dish won't crack later. Make sure, too, that you have enough clay to cut out the whole leaf. Place the leaf on the clay, with the textured side facing down.

2 Use the rolling pin to roll lightly over the leaf to ensure all the wonderful veins and other structures are imprinted in the clay. Cut out the leaf shape with the knife. Try holding the knife at a 90-degree angle to the surface of the clay, so the edges are as straight and neat as possible.

3 Remove the excess clay from around the leaf and then carefully peel the leaf away to reveal the delicate pattern on the surface of the clay.

4 Use a bowl that is about the same size as your leaf cutout. Carefully place the leaf inside the bowl and mold it into shape. I recommend lining the bowl with some baking paper first to prevent the clay from sticking. Let the leaf dry in this position.

5 Once the dish is completely dry, which might take one or two days depending on the thickness of the clay and the weather, you can decorate it. Use spray paint to spray the whole leaf, or regular watercolor paint and a paintbrush (as I did) to highlight the texture and give the dish a bit of color. If you want to set the paint afterward and make the dish washable, apply clear lacquer spray.

Trinket dishes can be used all around the house and also make great Christmas gifts. I have one in my hallway for my keys, and it makes me happy every time I come home. This craft project is also highly versatile, so you can experiment as much as you like—for example, you could leave the leaf white, use a black marker pen to highlight the delicate structures of the leaf in black, or get all artsy with several colors and shades to really capture the beauty of fall leaves.

CONKER WREATH

I love collecting conkers and acorns, and you can always find at least one in the pockets of my coat in the fall. I was looking for a pretty way to display them—and not just in an old jar. So, I came up with the idea of this wreath. It is easy to make and you can use it to decorate your door or a fall/winter table. The wreath will also last a very long time, and you can even keep it for the following season.

TOOLS AND MATERIALS

- Fall treasures, such as conkers, acorns, and pine cones
- Large piece of cardboard
- Small and large plates
- Pencil
- Scissors
- Hot-glue gun or craft glue
- Twine or ribbon (optional)

1 Collect all the pretty treasures you can find in the fall and let them dry out properly. If the conkers, for example, are fresh out of their shells, they need to dry out a bit, or they might start to go moldy in the wreath. Let them sit on a table or tray for a day or so after you bring them home.

2 Make the ring base for the wreath out of cardboard, drawing around the two plates with a pencil to create two concentric circles. I used a large and small kitchen plate to draw my inner and outer circles. Since cardboard is not that sturdy, I cut out two rings so I could reinforce the base. You can make your wreath as large as you wish, but I would avoid a diameter bigger than a large dinner plate or it will become too heavy.

3 Now glue the two cardboard rings together. It is a good idea to turn one of the rings 90 degrees, so the cardboard is going in a different direction in each layer. This will make the base even stronger. If you are planning to hang the wreath, place a length of looped twine or ribbon between the two layers and glue it securely inside.

4 Begin gluing your treasures onto the base, starting a little way from the top. Arrange a few pieces first and when you are happy with the display, lift them one by one and glue them to the base or to each other. You want to work in layers to make the wreath look more interesting and to hide as much of the cardboard as possible. I used mainly conkers and bigger pine cones as a base layer and then glued acorns and smaller pine cones on top.

5 Once you have worked your way around the base and are nearly back where you started gluing, look at the wreath to see where there are any gaps and then decide what you can add to finish off and make it look balanced. If there is still cardboard showing, especially on the inside of the ring (which can be difficult to cover completely), peel off small layers of pine cones and glue them as extra details to cover the gaps.

If you are a minimalist or have a specific color scheme in your home, you could spray the whole wreath at the end with some spray paint in a color of your choice. That way, you can create a very modern impression, especially if you use silver, gold, or even pink paint.

You could also add a nice ribbon to the top if you want your wreath to have a more festive look for Christmas. Then just remove the ribbon later to give the wreath more of a forest feel for the fall.

INDEX